First Ladies

Hillary Clinton

Jennifer Strand

Launch!
An Imprint of Abdo Zoom
abdopublishing.com

abdopublishing.com

Published by Abdo Zoom, a division of ABDO, PO Box 398166, Minneapolis, Minnesota 55439.

Printed in the United States of America, North Mankato, Minnesota.

052018
092018

THIS BOOK CONTAINS RECYCLED MATERIALS

Photo Credits: Alamy, AP Images, Getty Images, Seth Poppel/Yearbook Library, Shutterstock

Production Contributors: Kenny Abdo, Jennie Forsberg, Grace Hansen, John Hansen

Design Contributors: Dorothy Toth, Neil Klinepier

Library of Congress Control Number: 2017960625

Publisher's Cataloging-in-Publication Data

Names: Strand, Jennifer, author.

Title: Hillary Clinton / by Jennifer Strand.

Description: Minneapolis, Minnesota : Abdo Zoom, 2019. | Series: First ladies | Includes online resources and index.

Identifiers: ISBN 9781532122835 (lib.bdg.) | ISBN 9781532123818 (ebook) | ISBN 9781532124303 (Read-to-me ebook)

Subjects: LCSH: Clinton, Hillary Rodham 1947-, Biography--Juvenile literature. | Presidents' spouses--United States--Biography--Juvenile literature. | First ladies (United States)--Biography--Juvenile literature.

Classification: DDC 973.9290 [B]--dc23

Table of Contents

Introduction

Hillary Rodham Clinton was a First Lady of the United States. She is also a well-known **politician**.

Early Life

Hillary was born on October 26, 1947 in Chicago, Illinois. She swam and played softball in school.

Hillary was on the **debate** team in high school. She was a good public speaker.

Hillary supported children's **rights** in college. She then became a lawyer.

Leader

She married Bill Clinton in 1975. Their daughter Chelsea was born in 1980. Bill became **governor** of Arkansas in 1983.

Hillary worked with Bill to create better education and health care for the people of Arkansas.

She worked as a lawyer at the same time. No other First Lady of Arkansas had worked before her.

First Lady

Clinton was First Lady of the United States from 1993 to 2001.

She fought for women's **rights**. She also gave her husband advice.

Clinton also pressed for changes to health care laws. But **Congress** objected to her ideas.

Legacy

Clinton became a US **senator** in 2001. She then worked for President Barack Obama as **Secretary of State.**

Hillary ran for president in 2008 and 2016. She was the first woman elected to run for a major political party.

Quick Stats

Hillary Clinton

Born: October 26, 1947

Birthplace: Chicago, Illinois

Husband: Bill Clinton

Years Served: 1993–2001

Political Party: Democratic

Known For: Clinton was a US First Lady, a US senator, and a presidential candidate.

Key Dates

1947: Hillary Diane Rodham is born on October 26.

1975: Hillary and Bill Clinton are married.

1993–2001: Hillary Clinton is First Lady. Bill Clinton is the 42nd US president.

2000: Hillary Clinton is elected to the US Senate.

2009: Clinton becomes President Barack Obama's secretary of state.

2016: Hillary runs for president a second time.

Glossary

Congress – the body that makes the laws for the United States. It includes the House of Representatives and the Senate.

debate – when two people argue an idea or question in a public and formal setting.

governor – a person who is the head of a state in the United States.

rights – things people can have or do according to the law.

secretary of state – a person who runs the state department. They are responsible for foreign affairs.

senator – someone who is elected to make laws in the senate.

Online Resources

Booklinks
NONFICTION NETWORK
FREE! ONLINE NONFICTION RESOURCES

For more information on
Hillary Clinton, please visit
abdobooklinks.com

Abdo Zoom
DATABASES
BEGINNING ONLINE RESEARCH

Learn even more with the
Abdo Zoom Biographies database.
Visit **abdozoom.com** today!

Index